Really Short Walks to Explore Dartmoor

Paul White and Robert Hesketh

Bossiney Books

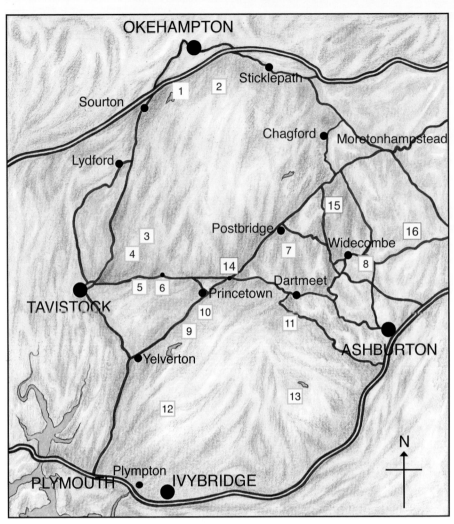

The approximate locations of the walks in this book

First published 2019 by
Bossiney Books Ltd, 67 West Busk Lane, Otley, LS21 3LY
www.bossineybooks.com

This book uses material from *Really Short Walks – North Dartmoor* and
Really Short Walks – South Dartmoor, but all walks have been checked.

ISBN 978-1-906474-79-9

Acknowledgements
The maps are by Graham Hallowell. All photographs are by Robert Hesketh –
www.roberthesketh.co.uk – or from the publisher's own collection.

Printed in Great Britain by Deltor, Saltash PL12 6LZ

Introduction

The walks in this book are approximately 2.3-5.7 km (1 1/2-3 1/2 miles) in length. Some are easy, others are short but quite challenging, so you may need to be selective. They have been chosen to show you some of the pleasures of Dartmoor and its landscapes, from its 'wilderness' qualities to the delightful countryside on its borders. Many of them also include places of interest – particularly prehistoric features and the remains of Dartmoor's ancient industries, especially mining.

For more background information about these features, please see our other books, *Ancient Dartmoor* and *Dartmoor's History*.

Footwear

The range of surfaces you will meet on short Dartmoor walks is much the same as you would meet on long walks. Ideally, therefore, wear walking boots – certainly not sandals! On most walks you will encounter at least one wet or muddy patch, and many more after a period of rain. Walking any distance in wellington boots is not recommended but a single short walk of under 5 km shouldn't cause a problem for most people – except be careful not to twist an ankle, since wellingtons provide no support and the ground is often uneven.

Maps

The sketch-maps in this book are just that – sketches. Anyone walking on the moor should take the Ordnance Survey's Dartmoor map, OL28.

Safety

Dartmoor requires respect. Its hills attract low cloud and within the cloud visibility can be abruptly reduced to a few metres. It can be damp, chilly and disorientating. Even for the shortest walk on the high moor, most regular walkers always carry a map and compass, a rucksack to contain extra clothing, a waterproof, and a bottle of water.

Some parts of the moor are used by the military and live firing takes place. The boundaries of the three 'ranges' are clearly marked by posts. Flags are flown on prominent tors when the range is in use. At weekends, peak holiday periods and on many other days the ranges are (generally) open to the public and they include some of the wildest parts of the moor. Details of the firing programme are available on-line, or as a recorded message if you phone 0800 458 4868.

Do take care if you go with children that they know not to pick up any strange object – though we have yet to see anything of the kind.

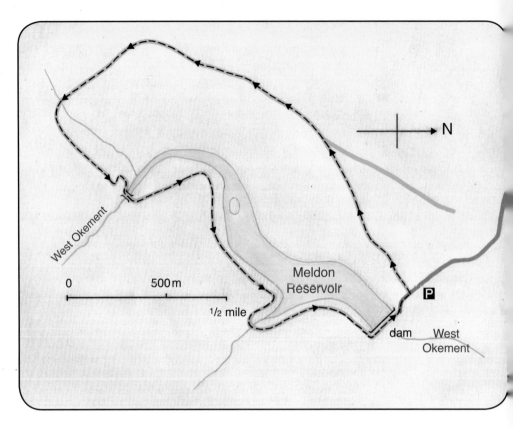

Walk 1 Meldon Reservoir

Length: 5.7km (3½ miles)
Character: This very scenic walk incudes good views of Sourton Tors,
Corn Ridge and the Okement valley, as well as Meldon Reservoir. There
is one steady ascent and one steeper descent, plus a small stream to cross.

To get there: From the eastbound A30, turn left to the B3260 signed
OKEHAMPTON. (There is no comparable turn westbound, so you need
to go up to the A386 and return a short way along the eastbound
carriageway.) Turn right through Meldon village, then turn left and
left again into the reservoir car park at SX562918.

Leave the car park by the steps next to the toilet block. Take the PUBLIC
BRIDLEWAY at the gate opposite and continue uphill. Reaching a junction of paths, continue ahead as signed.

Emerging onto open moor, walk ahead with the wall on your left.
Continue parallel to the wall when it curves left. Descend to cross a

stream. Bear left, veering away from the stream and the valley, but keeping to the upper contour of the slope on a grassy path to avoid marshy ground. Continue ahead and then downhill as the path zig-zags to the foot of the slope.

Turn right and descend to a footbridge over the River Okement. Cross and turn left on reaching a path. At a path junction, keep left on the lower path.

Continue ahead with the fence on your left as the path circuits the south bank of the reservoir. Turn left to cross the dam. Follow the lane ahead from the far end of the dam to the start.

Meldon Reservoir

This is the most recent Dartmoor reservoir, constructed – despite major opposition – in 1970. Water, like china clay and granite, is a Dartmoor resource which generates local controversy.

Meldon Viaduct

One of the most spectacular railway features of the south-west, this viaduct was built in 1874 as part of the LSWR line from Okehampton to Plymouth. It rises 36 m (118 ft) above the West Okement River and can be crossed by walkers and cyclists: trains run from Okehampton Station to the east end of the viaduct.

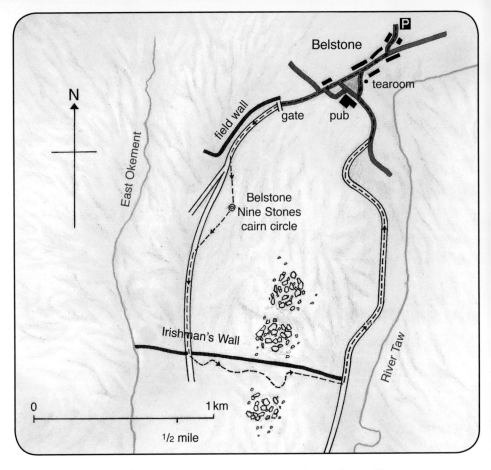

Walk 2 Belstone Nine Stones and Irishman's Wall

Length: 5.5 km (3¹/₂ miles)
Character: Quite tough going in places, over rough terrain, with one steep ascent and descent. Wonderful scenery, with a feel of the wild moor, and an interesting 'stone circle' – which is actually the remains of a burial cairn. The walk stops well short of the military firing range.

To get there: Take the Sticklepath road B3260 east from Okehampton, cross the A30 and take the second on the right to Belstone. Park in the main village car park (SX621939).

Turn left out of the car park into the attractive village, keeping right at the stocks, and then right again to pass the 'telegraph office', immediately keeping left up the hill on the 'main' lane for 300 m. Pass the waterworks, go through the gate and follow the track until the wall on the right turns away from the track.

6

At this point a lesser track bears off to the right of the main track. Don't follow either of them! Instead, bear off 30° to the left of the main track (i.e. approximately 11 o'clock from it, see sketch-map) heading towards a distant valley. After about 200 m you will see the Belstone Nine Stones. Now bear right, slightly downhill, to rejoin the track you were following. Keep to the main track.

After about 800m, and just before another track joins from the right, you will reach the ruins of a wall which crosses at right angles. It is very ruined, so not absolutely obvious. This is Irishman's Wall, said to have been built around 1820 as the northern boundary of a huge enclosure, which would have cut off Okehampton Commons from the moor. Okehampton's inhabitants went out at night and demolished it, after which the Irishmen took the hint – or so 'tis said!

Turn left beside the wall, and climb to the top of the ridge ahead of you by whatever path you choose. (The ground to the right of the wall is a little less rocky than the direct route.)

Once at the top, use the view as an excuse for a breather, then make your way down the other side, again by whatever route you choose: take care, as it would be easy to turn an ankle. In summer there's usually a bracken-free path near the wall.

A track runs between the ridge and the serpentine twistings of the infant River Taw. Turn left along it. After about 1km, pass through a gate and keep left along a tarmac lane to the village. At a fork turn right back to your car – unless of course you prefer to visit the tea-room or the pub first.

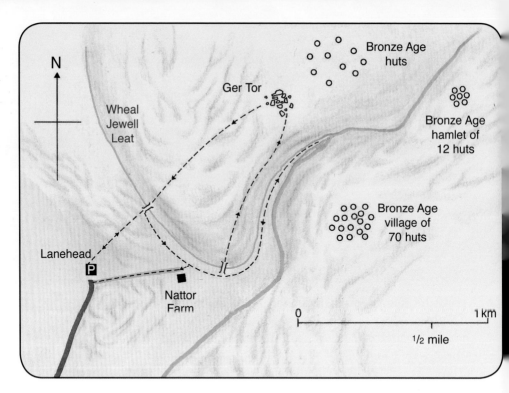

Walk 3   Tavy Cleave

Length: Each walk is approximately 3.5 km (2 miles).

Character: Two walks for the price of one! Walk A is virtually flat, there-and-back. Walk B is circular and quite strenuous. Both venture into Dartmoor's most dramatic river valley. Wild and desolate though it may now seem, in the Bronze Age the surrounding hillsides were dotted with large and presumably prosperous settlements.

Access: These walks are within the Willsworthy military range, which is the most used of the three Dartmoor ranges. An enormous red flag flies in the car park on firing days, so there is no risk that you won't know. Access is generally allowed throughout August, and at weekends, except for the weekend including the second Sunday in the month. It is worth checking the firing plan online, or by phoning 0800 458 4868 where a recorded message will detail the planned firing days, because other non-firing days do occur.

To get there: From Mary Tavy, follow the brown signs for the Elephant's Nest pub at Horndon, then follow signs for Willsworthy and then Lane End. There is a large car park (SX 537823).

8

Both walks: From the car park head for the prominent rocky hilltop ahead of you, which is Ger Tor. A well-beaten path leads from the flagpole up a gentle slope to a leat: turn right along this side of the leat.

Walk A: Continue along the footpath this side of the leat, which curves round to go up the valley. You will reach a concrete sluice. Turn back here. On your return, you can take a short cut (see map).

Walk B: Walk along this side of the leat to the next concrete bridge. Cross this and take the path uphill. At the top of the first ridge you will get a magnificent view of Tavy Cleave and the surrounding hills. Now head for the top of Ger Tor. On a good day you will get extensive views; you should be able to see your car and the Willsworthy farms to the south-west.

There is a scattering of Bronze Age hut circles about 200 m to the north-west of Ger Tor, and you may want to explore these. You may also be able to trace the remains of ancient field walls, known as 'reaves'.

Find a route down through the clitter (scattered boulders) on the west side of the tor. Pick up a beaten path which becomes ever more distinct as it nears the leat and returns to the car park.

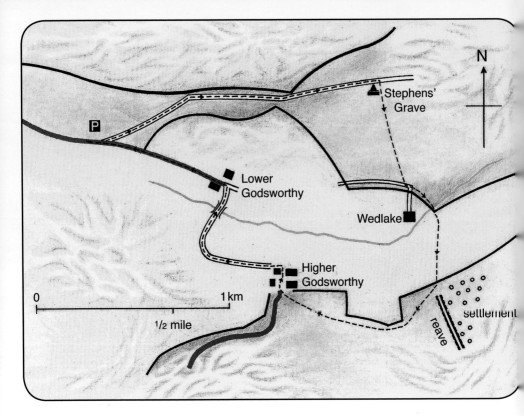

Walk 4 Peter Tavy

Length: 5 km (3 1/4 miles)
*Character: Beautiful scenery on the edge of the open moor, with a
large Bronze Age settlement to explore.*

*To get there: Peter Tavy lies 3 km north of Tavistock , just off the
A386. Turn right across Harford Bridge, then turn left into and
through the village. Pass the church on your left; 100 m further on,
turn right into a narrow lane. After 800 m, a disused quarry on the left
serves as a car park (SX 522779).*

Turn left out of the car park, and after 100 m bear left up a stony track.
After climbing steadily for 1.4 km you will reach Stephens' Grave:
George Stephens of Peter Tavy committed suicide in 1762, appar-
ently after being jilted, and was buried after the grisly fashion which
religion in those days required, at this remote moorland crossroads.

Turn right here along a grassy track. When you reach a wall, turn
left along it. Don't take the metalled track into Wedlake farm but continue along the wall.

10

Descend to a stream and go through a gate (PUBLIC BRIDLEPATH); follow the signs. Just to your left as you leave the enclosure through a field gate is an extensive Bronze Age village which is well worth exploring – some 70 or more huts, so probably a town by the standards of 3500 years ago, and intriguingly they all lie to the east of a massively broad 'reave' or stone hedge. Return to the gateway.

From the gateway, you need to bear right towards the prominent corner of the enclosure walls, where there is a solitary diminutive hawthorn tree.

Follow the path along the uphill side of the enclosure wall. When the wall turns abruptly away, bear right along the lower path – towards Brent Tor if visibility allows you to see it!

Join a tarmac lane to Higher Godsworthy. Turn left at the cattle grid as signed. Turn right at the gate 30 m ahead. Continue behind the farmhouse to a second gate. Turn left onto the farm track which leads to Lower Godsworthy.

Here you turn left onto a tarmac lane which will lead you back to your car.

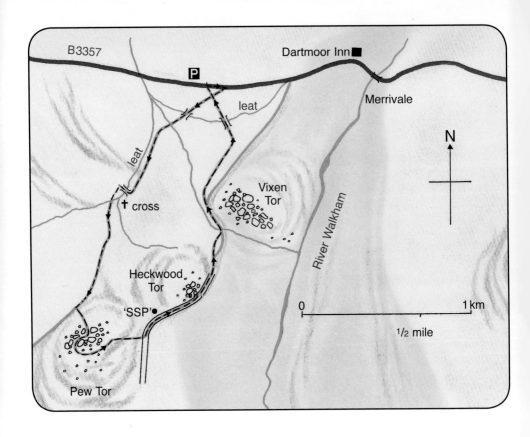

Walk 5 Vixen Tor and Pew Tor

Length: 4.5 km (2³/₄ miles)

Character: Beautiful open moorland and impressive tors, but mostly within sight of the main road across the moor, so relatively easy for navigation. Map and compass are nevertheless desirable, and essential in poor visibility: expect the going to be damp underfoot in places.

To get there: Coming from Tavistock, use a car park (SX539750) on the left of the road 1.1 km (0.7 miles) from the cattle grid which marks the start of the 40 mph zone. From Princetown, it is on the right at the top of the hill above Merrivale.

From the car park, turn left along the road for 100m. Turn sharp right at a small wooden post (PUBLIC FOOTPATH). Head south-west, aiming for the right of Feather Tor. (NB do **not** follow the path ahead towards Vixen Tor.) Cross a leat, then a stream, after which the path forks. Bear right and slightly uphill.

12

On reaching another leat, turn left along a path parallel to the near side. Enjoy the changing aspect of Vixen Tor away to your left.

The leat forks at a medieval cross. Just before the fork, cross the leat by a clapper bridge, then use stepping stones to cross the lower branch. Continue South-South-West along what is mainly a well trodden path, heading towards the right side of Pew Tor. Then take a clear path which branches left towards the top of the tor, from which there are panoramic views.

Descend the tor – see the sketch-map for what may be the best way down, and swing round to head East, towards the television mast at Princetown.

Lower down the slope you will see a track snaking along by a wall. Head down to join this track and follow it with the wall on the right, passing a boundary stone (SSP = Sampford Spiney parish) and several small disused quarries which the track once served.

Various paths descend a slope to cross a stream about 40m from the wall. Bear left to pass the corner of the wall. The car park is now due North, in the direction of Middle Staple Tor, but the path towards it diverts round to the right of some difficult ground – just how far to the right you go will depend on how much rainfall there has been recently.

Cross the clapper over a leat and walk up to the road.

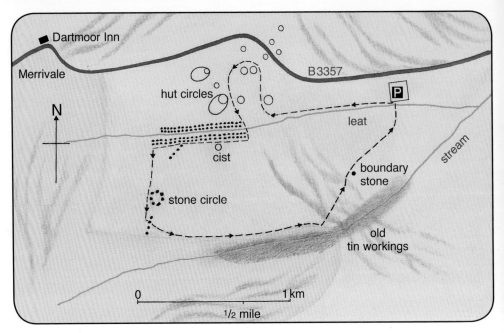

Walk 6 Merrivale

Length: 2.25 km (1 1/2 miles)
Character: A very short walk indeed, but absolutely packed with interest – a Bronze Age village, a ceremonial site with multiple stone rows, a circle and other features, as well as evidence of past tin-streaming and granite extraction.

To get there: Take the B3357 from Tavistock towards Princetown. After passing the Dartmoor Inn at Merrivale, climb the hill for 800m (1/2 mile) and you'll find a car park on the right surrounded by trees. Park here (SX561749).

Go through the gap in the back of the car park – it may be hard to believe, but this site was once a school. Don't cross the leat (artificial watercourse) but turn right along it. You will soon see two double stone rows, running away from you down the slope.

About 100m short of the rows, bear off to the right to explore the hut circles between the leat and the road. This Bronze Age village actually extends some distance beyond the road so it was quite substantial: as the weather was warmer and drier than it is now, it may have been possible to grow crops, as well as herding sheep and cattle. Some of the huts have pounds around them, either as farmyards or perhaps as vegetable gardens.

14

Now return to the top end of the stone rows – the leat runs between them. The further row has more features. Just to the left of it is a cist (a stone coffin, which would have been covered with a cairn of stones or earth) and another cairn lies in the middle of the row. There are at least 17 burial cairns in this vicinity, but it is uncertain whether the ceremonial site began as a funerary monument, or whether later generations thought it a holy place in which to bury their leaders. A shorter stone row, most of its stones buried, bears off to the left from a cairn at its head.

When you reach the end of the double row, clearly marked by two uprights, turn 90° left towards the great rock-strewn mass of King's Tor, and you will find a low stone circle and a standing stone, with yet another stone row, this time truncated.

Now bear left, following the wall down towards Long Ash Brook, a typical example of the landscape left by tin streaming. Streaming was rather like panning for gold: a great deal of waste was moved in the process, and left in spoil heaps.

Follow the top edge of the streamed valley until you reach an old track. Now head back uphill towards the car park with its trees, passing a standing stone marked 'T' on one side and 'A' on the other. This was one of a series of waymarks on the medieval route between Tavistock and Ashburton, long before there were any recognisable roads across the moor.

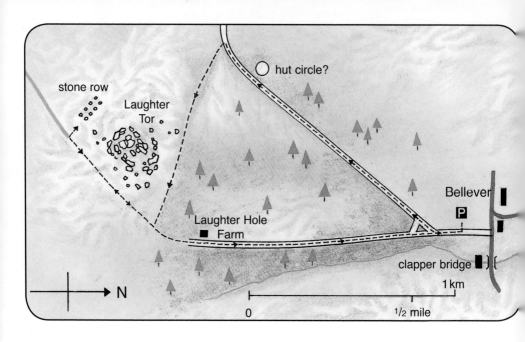

Walk 7   Bellever Forest

Length: 3.7km (2¹/₄ miles) or optionally 4.9km (3 miles)
Character: Easy walking with a long but gentle ascent and descent,
partly through conifer forest, partly open moorland.

To get there: From Postbridge on the B3212, start heading towards
Princetown, then almost immediately turn left. On reaching a
T-junction in Bellever, turn left and after 100m turn right into a large
car park within the wood. Start the walk from the notice board on the
verandah of the public toilets – how many loos can boast a verandah?
(You could as an alternative take the Forestry Commission waymarked
walk of 4km, which stays within the woodland.)

Walk forward to the track and turn right, initially following the red-
striped waymarks. Turn right through the picnic area, through the
gate at the end and up the track ahead of you, still following the red
waymarks, and climb steadily to the edge of the plantation. Shortly
before you reach that point, there is a small clearing on the right
containing what may be the remains of a hut circle – though even the
experts are unsure.

   When the track, with its waymarks, turns off to the right, you go over
a stile beside a field gate onto the moor. Turn left and keeping close to
the wall climb to the ridge of Laughter Tor, then continue down the

16

Bellever Tor from near Laughter Tor on the extension walk

The river near the picnic area

other side until a track crosses your route. Turn left to BELLEVER unless you want to take the extension (DUNNABRIDGE POUND).

Extension: Turn right along the track for 450 m. This will bring you to a double stone row some 50 m to the right of the path, which should be visible even above the summer vegetation. Most of the stones have been robbed out, but originally it led to the longstone in the distance, over 160 m away. Now retrace your steps.

Taking the BELLEVER route, go through the gate and after 100m keep right down a rough track. At the foot of the slope go straight on through Laughter Hole Farm, from which a long straight track brings you back to the picnic area. Keep right and follow the waymarked track back to your car.

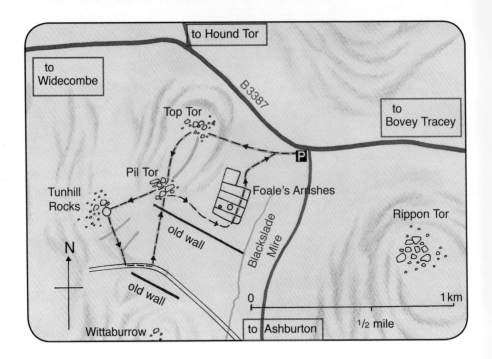

Walk 8   Foales Arrishes

Length: 3 km (2 miles)
Character: Two gentle ascents and descents are rewarded by stunning
panoramic views. Archaeological remains (far more complex than
shown on the sketch-map) add to the interest. Compass essential. Wear
long trousers because of gorse and brambles.

To get there: Take the B3387 from Bovey Tracey towards Widecombe.
The signpost at the Ashburton junction carries the name Hemsworthy
Gate; there's a parking area on the left just beyond the junction.

From the small parking area, follow the well beaten path to Top Tor.
The stone lines on your left are part of Foale's Arrishes. Bracken and
gorse partly hide their features, except when reduced by swaling (con-
trolled burning). Nothing hides the views from Top Tor. Rippon Tor
and Saddle Tor to the east and the Hameldown Ridge to the west are
especially impressive. Widecombe's lofty church tower, deep in the
valley below, is dwarfed by this magnificent scenery.

Walk SSW on one of the well beaten paths to Pil Tor. Bear WSW to
Tunhill Rocks, where the foundations of a single prehistoric circular
hut and its boundary wall are very clear.

18

Follow the path SSE across Blackslade Down towards Wittaburrow until it meets a broad, stony track. Turn left onto the track. (The line of stones ahead is just a wall, not a stone row.) As the track begins to curve away to the right, turn left up another rough path to Pil Tor.

Aim for the right side of the tor, then pick your way carefully East over rough ground to take a closer look at Foale's Arrishes. The field boundaries are the most obvious feature. The hut circles will take some finding except in the winter months. Explore the area and hopefully you will find the path, which heads slightly to the left of the car park area. The lower ground is boggy.

> **Foale's Arrishes**
>
> 'Arrish' is a Devon word for a cornfield, and Foale was the last landlord of the New Inn at Hemsworthy Gate, which was demolished in the 1830s, but the arrishes are much older than that. This is a very complex site. The main banks and walls we can see today – though only when vegetation allows – probably date from around 1700 BC, but they replaced an even earlier field system.
>
> Eight hut circles have been found within the settlement, but you will be very lucky to spot any of them. Unusually there is evidence of occupation in the Iron Age, then of medieval re-occupation, and then again of early 19th century newtakes being added.
>
> The planning and workmanship of the Bronze Age walls is far superior to that of the 19th century newtakes!

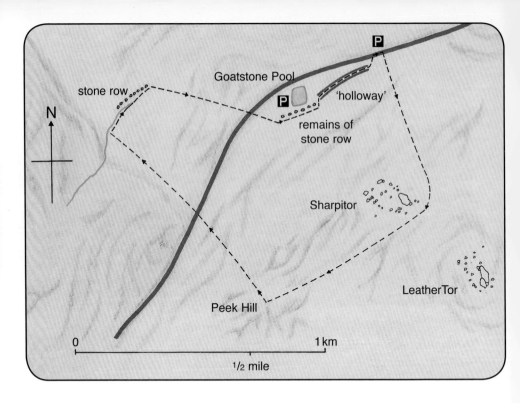

Walk 9   Around Sharpitor

Length: 4km (2¹/₂ miles)
*Character: Magnificent scenery, together with some interesting
ancient features. You will need a compass to follow the directions, and
preferably an OS map for safety on this open moorland.*

*To get there: From Yelverton, take the Princetown road. It climbs for
5km (3 miles). When you start to descend from the first crest, you will
see a car park on the left (SW 560709).*

Cross the road from the car park. You will see a tor ahead of you –
Sharpitor. Walk towards it, then leave the path to pass the tor about
100 m to its left. You will soon cross the remains of a substantial old
wall – a very old wall. It was one of two parallel 'reaves' which sepa-
rated two Bronze Age communities about 3500 years ago, with a strip
of no-man's land, 350 m wide, between them.

As you skirt round Sharpitor, you will see what looks like a natural
pyramid ahead of you, which is Leather Tor. Another reave runs
between them. From the saddle halfway between Sharpitor and
Leather Tor there is a magnificent view over Burrator Reservoir.

Follow the contour gently upwards towards Peek Hill. Climb to the top, where there are two cairns, one badly damaged, the other a mound with a concrete pit on the summit – perhaps the remains of a military building of some kind.

Now head North-West, which brings you down to the road. Cross it just above an enclosure with trees growing from its stone wall. Continue North-West, roughly parallel to the wall, till you reach a streamlet (liable to run dry in summer). Turn right up its near side. After 100 m, a waist-high stone marks the lower end of a stone row, about 130 m in length. At the upper end you will find a cairn, but so ruined and hidden in bracken as to be scarcely recognisable.

From this point bear right, and head just to the left of Sharpitor, on the horizon. If there are cars on the road, head for the uphill point where they go out of sight – it's approximately 110° if you're expert with the compass.

Cross the road and turn left along it. At the summit you'll find Goatstone Pool, with a car park. There are actually two more stone rows here, but you need either experience or imagination to spot both of them! From the back of the pool, walk parallel to the road, and you should find an old track (a 'holloway'). This was, I believe, part of the main road across the moor from Plymouth to Exeter, from Roman times until the road was turnpiked around 1812. Keep to the left of it to return to the car park.

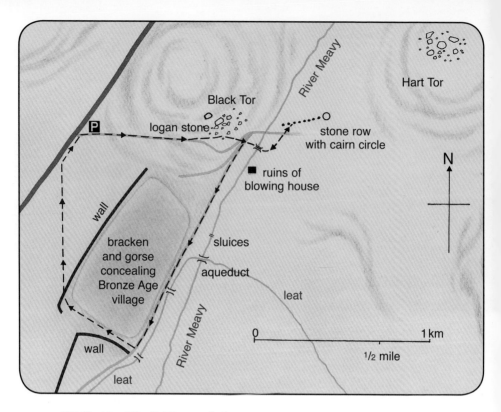

Walk 10   Black Tor and the River Meavy

Length: 2.8 km (1³/₄ miles)

Character: An extremely short walk, but with masses of interest – a logan stone, a double stone row, the ruins of a Tudor tin stamping and smelting area, a leat with miniature aqueduct, as well as glorious scenery. A compass might be useful.

To get there: finding the right parking place is tricky. It is a small layby on the east side of the B3212, 2.7 km (1.7 miles) from the mini-roundabout in Princetown – or 6.6 km (4.1 miles) from the Yelverton roundabout. Black Tor is not visible from the layby.

Head east, away from the road, on a broad track, then divert left up to Black Tor. Notice the logan stone – a chunk of granite resting just on one point: 'logging' is a dialect word for rocking, and some such rocks do so, but I wouldn't recommend trying – they're sometimes called nutcracker rocks. From the far (East) end of the main outcrop, head downhill over rough ground to where you can cross the stream by a metal plank – but only if conditions allow you to do so safely.

22

The other side is boggy, so go a few metres to the right for the easiest route, then turn back upstream, mount the bank and turn left. You will reach an attractive double stone row, leading up to a cairn. It has been standing here for about 3500-4000 years.

Retrace your steps to cross the metal plank, then turn left. At a junction, keep left to follow the bank. The ruins on either side of the stream were tin 'blowing houses' (photo above), possibly 16th century, workshops for extracting tin from its ore by 'stamps', 'buddles', and then furnaces, using water power.

Walk roughly parallel to the river to a bridge – though when you get closer you will see that in fact it is an aqueduct.

The Devonport leat rushes down Raddick Hill on the other side, crosses the River Meavy, then turns sharp left. Continue with the leat on your left for 450m, to a point where a substantial wall descends from the right, and a broad footbridge crosses the leat.

Turn right, passing a massive gatepost and then keeping the wall on your left. When the path forks, keep right uphill and head north by one of many transient paths through the bracken and gorse.

When the TV mast comes in sight, head in that direction, then cross a wall to your left and head across to the road. This area can be boggy in places after rain, so you might need to adapt your route according to conditions underfoot.

On reaching the road, turn right, back to your car.

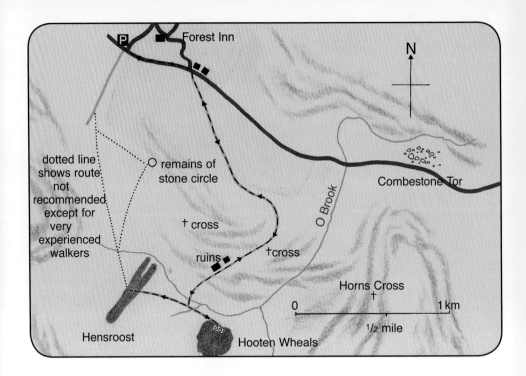

Walk 11 Hooten Wheals

Length: 5.9 km (3¾ miles) or including Hensroost 6.7 km (4¼ miles)
Character: This is a there-and-back walk, but visiting some of
Dartmoor's most interesting mining remains, as well as safely visiting
some of the moor's more daunting scenery.

To get there: From the Two Bridges-Ashburton Road, 1 km (½ mile)
west of Dartmeet, turn South, towards Hexworthy and Holne. Cross
Hexworthy Bridge and climb steeply. Pass the Forest Inn and then after
a further hair-pin bend turn sharp right towards SHERBERTON. After
500 m the lane opens onto a green. Park off-road at SX 651728.

Walk back along the road to the SHERBERTON sign. Walk in the HOLNE
direction for 10 m, then turn right across a stile, and join the track
uphill. At each gate there is a neighbouring stile not far away.

  Keep following the track. In time you will enter the open moor, and
pass a stone cross to your left. Then you will pass ruined buildings
on the right, one of which provided accommodation for the 30 or so
miners who worked here when production was at its peak: they came
from the edges of the moor, and went home at weekends.

  The track ends at a T-junction. Turn left and after 250m (usually

24

damp underfoot!) you will reach the tin-dressing floors of Hooten Wheals, which you may well want to explore – but be very cautious. Old mine sites are dangerous places.

Now return to the T-junction. If you want to include Hensroost in the walk, carry straight on up what was once a tramway, but is now trying to become a watercourse! At the top you will reach a quite monstrous gully, all dug out by hand over many generations.

Now return again to the T-junction. (The direct route back is over difficult ground and suitable only for very experienced moorland walkers.) Retrace your steps down the track and back to your car.

Hooten Wheals

This is the older name of a mine which was later worked along with the Hensroost under the name Hexworthy Mine. Tin streaming in this valley may date back to the time of King John. The earliest evidence for shaft-mining on the moor, probably in the 18th century, comes from this site. Most of what you can see dates from the reworking of the mine from 1890 to 1920.

The visible remains include 'buddles' – circular tanks which allowed solids of different density to separate, part of the process by which the tin was isolated from the waste products. The buddles you can see were only put in place in 1905, at which time a hydro-electric generator was also installed. As usual with Dartmoor mines, Hooten Wheals was for most of its life powered by waterwheels.

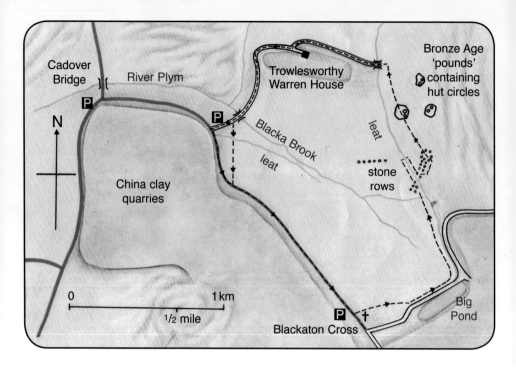

Walk 12   Trowlesworthy

Length: 5.2 km (3¹/₄ miles)
*Character: Despite its proximity to major china clay workings, and
the ice-cream vans at Cadover Bridge, the general impression is of open
and empty moorland. Two stone rows, an extensive Bronze Age settlement, and remains of tin mining add much to the interest of the walk.
Some parts can be a bit squelchy so waterproof footwear is needed.*

*To get there: From Cadover Bridge, on the road from Yelverton
towards Lee Moor, take the road up the valley, signed as a dead
end. Follow this for 2 km (1¹/₄ miles) and you will find a car park
(SX 570631) on the right just before Blackaton Cross – a roadside cross
with a medieval head and a replacement shaft.*

Opposite the car park there is a track. Walk towards a massive bank
of quarry waste. A quarry track runs along the bank with 'Big Pond'
beyond it. The track itself is out-of-bounds so walk parallel to it on
the lower level. When you reach a broad leat, turn left and make your
way along the near bank of the leat.

Cross a small overflow stream. Just beyond this is a double stone
row, cut in two by the leat. There is another stone row 150m further

on on the left. Cross the leat opposite that second row by a small stone clapper bridge. Return to the double row. At its top end you will find a stone circle, which is all that remains of a cairn. (Many stone rows have a cairn at their upper end, by no means just a heap of stones but often a complex monumental structure.)

From the cairn circle, continue along the hillside, parallel to the leat at 50-75 m from it. You will pass through both naturally occurring stone ('clitter') and several Bronze Age 'pounds'. Each pound was presumably a family farm and each contained hut circles. Some of them were for storage and some of them dwellings.

This is a fascinating and evocative hillside to explore, especially when the bracken has died down, say from late October to May. The largest pounds are actually a little further up the hill, 100-150m above the leat, and there are no fewer than 13 pounds in total.

Gradually get a little closer to the leat. Where it is crossed by a stony cart track, turn left and follow the track down past the upper side of Trowlesworthy Warren House and its enclosure, then join the farm's access track down to a bridge over the Blacka Brook at the point where it enters the Plym. The whole valley is full of tinners' mounds – ground which was worked for tin over many generations.

There is a car park here. You now have a choice: either follow the car park track to the road and turn left along it, or veer left (south) towards the long low man-made hill of quarry waste – the landscape of 'reclamation'. There is a narrow leat which is easily crossed, but the hillside above it does get waterlogged in winter. Turn left along the road back to your car.

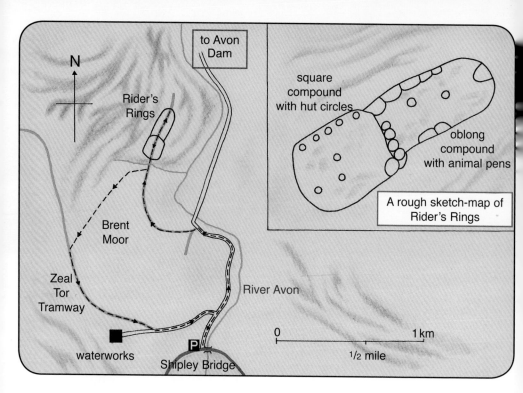

to Avon Dam

square
compound
with hut circles

oblong
compound
with animal pens

A rough sketch-map of
Rider's Rings

N

Rider's
Rings

Brent
Moor

Zeal
Tor
Tramway

River Avon

0   1 km

waterworks

1/2 mile

P

Shipley Bridge

Walk 13 Shipley Bridge and Rider's Rings

Length: 5.4km (3¹/₄ miles)
*Character: This walk starts with a gentle stroll beside the Avon with
its delightful freshets (rapids) and waterfalls, then climbs to Dartmoor's
second largest Bronze Age settlement, returning via the old Zeal Tor
Tramway. High open moor and rough ground – real Dartmoor!
Map and compass essential.*

*To get there: Shipley Bridge (SX 682628) with its popular car park is
signed on lanes from South Brent and Buckfastleigh.*

From Shipley Bridge follow the tarmac track upstream for 1 km. The
lane curves left. About 50m before it curves back right to cross the
Avon, turn sharp left up an unsigned and initially rocky path, which
soon divides. Bear right and follow the path diagonally up the hill.

Push on through the bracken to a gully, cut by a small stream. This
was the water source for the settlement ahead known as Rider's Rings.
Cross the stream and continue on the narrow path. Lines and circles
of stone, some overgrown with moss and bracken, mark this Bronze
Age pound, with its many huts and stock pens. However, when the

bracken is up (May to October) it is hard to tell what's what on the ground. Only the main walls are easily visible.

Retrace your steps to the gully. Recross the stream and head uphill, bearing left and away from the gully to reach the top of Brent Moor.

Take a SW bearing until you meet Zeal Tor Tramway, now a long linear feature – see photograph above. Turn left along the tramway. Its course is clear enough until just above a modern water treatment works. Continue in the same direction, above the gorse bushes which are thick and vigorous, to a tarmac track which leads to the works. Turn left, and walk down to rejoin the track you started on. Turn right along it.

The curious building with narrow vertical openings in the car park was once the drying shed for the china clay works. Up the slope to the left are the remains of the old clay settling pits.

Rider's Rings

The insert on the sketch-map gives a rough idea of the plan. Rider's Rings consists of two walled enclosures sharing a party wall. The western enclosure is almost square and seems to have been the living area. The other, larger and oblong, was added later and has numerous smaller animal pens along its wall – rather like the pens at animal auctions. The two enclosures jointly cover 2.5 hectares (six acres) and contain more than thirty buildings.

There-and-back walks

Walk 14 Wistman's Wood

This is an easy open moorland walk, 4km (2½ miles) in total, to a rare vestige of Dartmoor's primeval oak woodland. Park in the old quarry (SX609750) directly opposite the Two Bridges Hotel where the two main moorland roads, B3212 and B3357, intersect.

Walk north through a gate and follow the track to Crockern Farm. Keep right of the house and follow the well-used track along the side of the valley. A stile leads into the nature reserve and information boards describe the significance of the dwarf oaks and their unique lichens.

Boulders protect the gnarled and stunted oaks from both grazing animals and the depredations of mankind, which began with woodland clearances in the Mesolithic period, 7000 years ago. By 2000BC, people had destroyed most of Dartmoor's native woodland.

On the return, note Crockern Tor on your left. The fiercely independent Dartmoor tinners held their Stannary Parliament here. Asserting their legal rights, they even contested power with Westminster and imprisoned Richard Strode MP at Lydford Castle in 1512 when he objected to their Dartmoor tin workings silting up the River Plym. Sir Walter Raleigh was the most noted Lord Warden of the Stannaries, Plympton, Ashburton, Chagford and Tavistock being the Stannary towns where tin was weighed and assayed.

Walk 15 Grimspound

Grimspound, with its high double walled enclosure of 1.6 ha protecting 24 hut circles, is Dartmoor's most impressive prehistoric site.

At first glance, it looks like a fort, but its sheltered position in the Challacombe valley below Hameldown and Hookney Tors shows that it was built as a pound to keep domestic animals in and predators such as wolves and foxes out. With a little imagination, you can step back into the Bronze Age when Grimspound was built and sheltered a thriving community of perhaps fifty people, who herded sheep and cattle, grew crops (probably beans and oats) and hunted abundant game.

Park carefully on the layby at SX697809. Take the path uphill, GRIMSPOUND, for 400 m. (Parts of this path have been paved with granite flown in by helicopter.) Opposite Grimspound are the deep gullies dug by tin miners at Headland Warren and the field patterns created by medieval farmers at Challacombe village 1 km south.

Walk 16 Haytor granite tramway

The Haytor Granite Tramway ran downhill 400 m (1300 ft) from the Haytor Quarries to waiting barges on the river Teign at Teigngrace, 13.7 km (8½ miles) distant. Opened in 1820, it ran on hand-cut granite rails and used horse traction to haul the wagons back to the quarries. The best surviving section of the tramway can be followed on a near level course for 2.5 km (1½ miles) to the quarries west of Haytor Rocks, or along spurs to Holwell Quarry SX751778, or the strikingly beautiful and partly flooded Haytor Quarry SX761774.

The most convenient parking area, if approaching from Bovey Tracey on the B3387, is 100 m right on the minor road to Manaton at SX768775.

Some other Bossiney books about Dartmoor

Discover Dartmoor
Ancient Dartmoor
Dartmoor's History

Fairly Easy walks on Dartmoor (3-9 km walks)
Shortish Walks on Dartmoor (6-8 km walks)
Dartmoor Pub Walks (7-14 km walks)
Walks on High Dartmoor (7-20 km walks)